The Dividend Millionaire

A Step-by-Step Guide to Building Wealth through Dividend Investing

Mark O'Niel

The Dividend Millionaire

All rights reserved. No part of this publication may be reproduced, distributed, or transmitted in any form or by any means, including photocopying, recording, or other electronic or mechanical methods, without the prior written permission of the publisher, except in the case of brief quotations embodied in critical reviews and certain other noncommercial uses permitted by copyright law.

Copyright © Mark O'Niel, 2023.

Table of Contents

PART ONE
  The basics of dividend investing
  The Benefits of Dividend Investing

PART TWO
  How to find the best dividend-paying stocks
  Diversifying your dividend portfolio
  Reinvesting Dividends for Maximum Growth
  Tax considerations for dividend investors
  Managing risk in a dividend portfolio

PART THREE
  Advanced Strategies for Experienced Investors
  Case studies and real-world examples

PART ONE

The basics of dividend investing

Dividends are payments made by a corporation to its shareholders, typically in the form of cash or additional shares of stock. Dividends are typically paid on a regular basis, such as quarterly or annually, and are usually a percentage of the company's profits. Companies may choose to pay dividends for a variety of reasons, such as to distribute excess profits to shareholders, to attract and retain investors, or to demonstrate the company's financial stability and growth potential.

There are two main types of dividend-paying stocks: common stock and preferred stock. Common stock is the most widely owned type of stock, and holders of common stock are typically entitled to vote at shareholder meetings and have the potential to receive dividends. Preferred stock is a type of stock that typically pays a fixed dividend and has priority over common stock in terms of dividend payments and the liquidation of assets.

There are several factors that can impact the amount and frequency of dividends paid by a company. These include the company's profitability, its cash flow, its debt levels, and its future growth prospects. Companies with a strong financial track record and a history of consistent profits are more likely to pay dividends, while companies with weaker financials or uncertain futures may choose to retain their profits or pay smaller dividends.

In addition to traditional dividends, some companies also offer dividend reinvestment plans (DRPs) or dividend reinvestment and stock purchase plans (DRSPs). These plans allow shareholders to automatically reinvest their dividends in additional shares of the company's stock, rather than receiving the dividends in cash. This can be a useful way for investors to compound their returns and build a larger position in the company over time.

Dividend reinvestment plans (DRPs) and dividend reinvestment and stock purchase plans (DRSPs) plans are typically offered by companies as a way to allow shareholders to gradually build a larger position in the company over time, and they can be a useful way for investors to compound their returns and potentially earn higher returns over the long-term.

DRPs and DRSPs typically operate by allowing shareholders to enroll in the program and designate a specific bank account for the automatic reinvestment of dividends. When the company pays dividends, the dividends are automatically reinvested in additional shares of the company's stock, which are then credited to the shareholder's account. Some plans may also allow shareholders to purchase additional shares of the company's stock at a discounted price.

There are several potential benefits to using DRPs or DRSPs. One of the main benefits is the potential to compound returns over time. By reinvesting dividends in additional shares of stock, investors can potentially earn higher returns through the power of compound interest. For example, if a company's stock price appreciates over time, the value of the additional shares purchased through the dividend reinvestment plan will also increase. This can potentially lead to higher overall returns for the investor.

DRPs and DRSPs can also be a convenient way for investors to gradually build a position in a company without having to make large upfront investments. By reinvesting dividends over time, investors can potentially accumulate a larger position in the company without having to commit a large amount of capital upfront.

There are also tax considerations to be aware of when it comes to DRPs and DRSPs. In some cases, dividends received through these plans may be subject to capital gains taxes, rather than being taxed at the shareholder's regular income tax rate. It is important for investors to understand the tax implications of these plans and consult with a financial advisor or tax professional to determine the most tax-efficient way to invest.

While there are several potential benefits to using DRPs or DRSPs, it is important for investors to carefully consider their investment objectives and risk tolerance before enrolling in these programs. Some investors may prefer to receive dividends in cash, particularly if they need the income to meet short-term financial obligations or if they have concerns about the company's financial stability. Additionally, it is important for investors to understand that the value of their investment can fluctuate over time, and there is always the potential for loss.

There are also several different strategies that investors can use when it comes to dividend investing. Some investors focus on high-yield dividends, which are dividends that offer a higher percentage of the stock price. These types of dividends can be attractive for income-oriented investors who are looking for a steady stream of cash. Other investors focus on growth dividends, which are dividends that are expected to increase over time as the company's profits grow. These types of dividends can be attractive for investors who are looking for long-term capital appreciation. Some investors also focus on dividend income as a way to diversify their portfolio and generate a passive income stream.

There are also several exchange-traded funds (ETFs) and mutual funds that focus on dividend-paying stocks, which can be a useful way for investors to diversify their portfolio and access a broad range of dividend-paying stocks. These types of funds typically invest in a diverse selection of dividend-paying stocks and offer investors the benefits of professional management and diversification.

Exchange-traded funds (ETFs) and mutual funds that focus on dividend-paying stocks are a popular way for investors to access a broad range of dividend-paying stocks and diversify their portfolio. These types of funds typically invest in a diverse selection of dividend-paying stocks and offer investors the benefits of professional management and diversification.

One of the main advantages of dividend-focused ETFs and mutual funds is the ease of diversification. By investing in a single fund, investors can gain exposure to a wide range of dividend-paying stocks, which can help to reduce volatility and mitigate the impact of any individual stock's performance. This can be particularly useful for investors who may not have the time or expertise to build their own dividend-focused portfolio.

Another advantage of these types of funds is the ability to access a wide range of sectors and industries. Many dividend-focused ETFs and mutual funds invest in a variety of sectors, such as technology, healthcare, financials, and utilities, which can help to further diversify the portfolio and reduce risk.

In addition to diversification and sector exposure, dividend-focused ETFs and mutual funds can also offer the benefits of professional management. Many of these funds are managed by experienced professionals who have extensive knowledge of the dividend investing landscape and use rigorous research and analysis to identify attractive dividend-paying stocks.

There are also a variety of different types of dividend-focused ETFs and mutual funds available, each with its own unique investment strategy. Some funds focus on high-yield dividends, while others focus on growth dividends or a combination of both. Some funds also employ more advanced strategies, such as using options or other derivatives to enhance returns or hedge against risk.

Overall, dividend investing can be a powerful tool for building wealth and generating a passive income stream. By understanding the basics of dividends, how they are paid, and the different types of dividend-paying stocks, investors can make informed decisions and build a successful dividend investment strategy.

The Benefits of Dividend Investing

Potential for High Returns

One of the main benefits of dividend investing is the potential for high returns. Over the long term, dividend-paying stocks have historically outperformed non-dividend-paying stocks and the overall market. This is due in part to the fact that companies that pay dividends are typically more established and financially stable, which can lead to better stock performance. In addition, the dividend itself can provide an additional source of return for investors.

However, it is important to note that the potential returns of dividend investing are not guaranteed and will depend on a variety of factors, including the performance of the underlying stocks, market conditions, and economic conditions. Investors should carefully consider their own risk tolerance and financial goals before investing in dividend-paying stocks.

Passive Income Stream

Dividend investing can be an effective way to generate a passive income stream. By investing in dividend-paying stocks, investors can receive a regular payment of dividends, which can be used to supplement other income sources or to fund expenses. This can be particularly appealing for investors who are looking for a steady stream of income, such as retirees or those on a fixed income.

Many dividend-paying stocks have a long history of consistent dividend payments, and the dividends themselves are typically a percentage of the company's profits. This can provide a degree of predictability and stability compared to other types of investments, such as stocks that do not pay dividends or investments that are subject to market fluctuations.

However, it is important to note that the amount and frequency of dividends can vary based on a company's profitability, cash flow, and other factors. Some dividend-paying stocks may offer a higher yield, while others may offer a lower yield but the potential for faster dividend growth. Investors should carefully consider their own financial needs and goals when selecting dividend-paying stocks.

This can be particularly appealing for investors who are looking for a steady stream of income, such as retirees or those on a fixed income. It is important to note that the amount and frequency of dividends can vary based on a company's profitability, cash flow, and other factors. Some dividend-paying stocks may offer a higher yield, while others may offer a lower yield but the potential for faster dividend growth.

In addition to the potential for high returns and passive income, dividend investing also offers several other benefits. One of the main benefits is the diversification benefits. By investing in a variety of dividend-paying stocks, investors can spread their risk across different sectors and industries, which can help to reduce volatility and mitigate the impact of any individual stock's performance. Dividend investing can also be a useful way to generate income in a low-interest rate environment, as traditional fixed-income investments such as bonds may offer low yields.

Company Evaluation

Another benefit of dividend investing is the ability to evaluate a company's financial stability and growth prospects. There are several factors that can impact a company's ability to pay dividends, including profitability, cash flow, and debt levels. Companies with strong profitability and cash flow are more likely to be able to pay dividends, as they have the financial resources to do so. Companies with high levels of debt may be less likely to pay dividends, as they may need to use their profits to pay down debt rather than distributing them to shareholders.

Investors can also consider a company's management team, industry trends, and competitive position when evaluating its financial stability and growth prospects. Companies with strong management teams, favorable industry trends, and a competitive advantage in their market are typically seen as more likely to generate future growth.

There are several tools and resources that investors can use to evaluate a company's financial stability and growth prospects. One of the most common tools is financial statements, such as the balance sheet, income statement, and cash flow statement. These documents provide detailed information on a company's financial performance, including its revenue, expenses, profits, and debts. Investors can use this information to assess the company's financial health and determine whether it is likely to be able to pay dividends in the future.

Other resources that investors can use to evaluate a company's financial stability and growth prospects include analysts' reports, industry reports, and company presentations. These sources can provide valuable insights into a company's business model, competitive position, and growth prospects.

Risk Management

Finally, Dividends can be a useful way to manage risk in an investment portfolio in several ways. One of the main ways is through the diversification benefits of dividend investing. By investing in a variety of dividend-paying stocks, investors can spread their risk across different sectors and industries, which can help to reduce volatility and mitigate the impact of any individual stock's performance. This can be particularly useful for investors who may not have the time or expertise to build their own diversified portfolio.

Companies that are consistently profitable and able to pay dividends are typically seen as more financially stable and capable of generating future growth. This can provide a degree of comfort for investors who may be concerned about the stability of their portfolio.

With traditional fixed-income investments such as bonds offering low yields, many investors are turning to dividend-paying stocks as a way to generate a higher yield. Dividends can be a useful way to manage risk by providing a source of liquidity. By receiving dividends in cash, investors can use the funds to meet their short-term financial needs or to invest in other opportunities. This can be particularly useful for investors who may not want to sell their stocks in order to raise cash. By investing in a mix of dividend-paying stocks and other types of investments, investors can create a well-balanced portfolio that is more resilient to market fluctuations.

PART TWO

How to find the best dividend-paying stocks

Finding the best dividend-paying stocks can be a key component of a successful dividend investment strategy. By identifying companies that are financially stable, consistently profitable, and capable of generating future growth, investors can build a portfolio of high-quality dividend-paying stocks that can provide a reliable stream of passive income and potential for capital appreciation.

There are several strategies that investors can use when it comes to researching and evaluating dividend-paying stocks. One of the most important strategies is to analyze the company's financial statements. This includes reviewing the company's income statement, balance sheet, and cash flow statement to get a sense of its profitability, debt levels, and liquidity. By analyzing financial statements, investors can identify companies that are consistently profitable and have a strong financial foundation.

Another important strategy is to study the company's history. This includes looking at the company's track record of dividend payments, as well as its overall financial performance over time. Companies with a long history of consistent dividends and strong financial performance are typically seen as more reliable dividend payers.

In addition to financial analysis, it can also be helpful to consider industry trends and the company's competitive position within its industry. This can include analyzing the company's market share, product offerings, and competitive advantages. Companies that are leaders in their industry and have a strong competitive position are often better positioned to generate future growth and pay dividends.

Another important strategy is to diversify your dividend portfolio. By investing in a variety of dividend-paying stocks, investors can spread their risk across different sectors and industries, which can help to reduce volatility and mitigate the impact of any individual stock's performance.

Finally, it can also be helpful to consult with financial professionals such as financial advisors or investment analysts. These professionals can provide valuable insights and advice on the dividend investing landscape and help investors make informed decisions.

In addition to these strategies, there are also several resources available to help investors research and evaluate dividend-paying stocks. These resources include financial websites, news sources, and research firms that provide analysis and commentary on the stock market and individual companies. Many of these resources offer tools and resources such as stock screeners, which allow investors to filter and sort stocks based on various criteria such as dividends, financial metrics, and industry.

It is important to note that no investment is without risk, and dividend-paying stocks are no exception. While these types of stocks can offer the potential for high returns and a reliable stream of passive income, they can also fluctuate in value based on a variety of factors, including the performance of the underlying company, market conditions, and economic conditions. Investors should carefully consider their own risk tolerance and financial goals before investing in any dividend-paying stock.

Diversifying your dividend portfolio

Diversification is a key principle of investing, and it is especially important when it comes to dividend investing. By diversifying your dividend portfolio, you can spread your risk across different sectors and industries, which can help to reduce volatility and mitigate the impact of any individual stock's performance. In this section, we'll delve into strategies for building a diverse portfolio of dividend-paying stocks, including investing in a variety of industries and market sectors and balancing high-yield and growth stocks.

One of the main ways for diversifying your dividend portfolio is to invest in a variety of industries and market sectors. This can help to reduce the impact of any one sector's performance on your overall portfolio. For example, if you invest in a variety of sectors such as technology, healthcare, financials, and utilities, you can mitigate the impact of any one sector's performance on your overall portfolio. You can also consider investing in international dividend-paying stocks, which can provide further diversification and potentially reduce currency risk.

Another important way for diversifying your dividend portfolio is to balance high-yield and growth stocks. High-yield dividends are dividends that offer a higher percentage of the stock price, and they can be attractive for income-oriented investors who are looking for a steady stream of cash. Growth dividends, on the other hand, are dividends that are expected to increase over time as the company's profits grow. These types of dividends can be attractive for investors who are looking for long-term capital appreciation. By balancing high-yield and growth dividends, investors can create a well-rounded portfolio that is more resilient to market fluctuations.

It is also important to diversify within individual sectors and industries. For example, rather than investing in a single technology company, you could invest in a variety of technology companies that operate in different subsectors and have different business models. This can help to reduce the impact of any one company's performance on your portfolio.

In addition to investing in a variety of sectors and industries, investors can also consider diversifying their portfolio by investing in different types of dividend-paying stocks. This can include common stocks, preferred stocks, and dividend-paying ETFs and mutual funds. By investing in a mix of these different types of stocks, investors can further diversify their portfolio and potentially reduce risk.

It is also important to periodically review and rebalance your dividend portfolio. As market conditions and the performance of individual stocks change, it is important to ensure that your portfolio remains well-balanced and aligned with your financial goals. This may include selling some stocks and buying others, or adjusting the overall allocation of your portfolio. By regularly reviewing and rebalancing your portfolio, you can ensure that it remains diversified and well-positioned for long-term success.

In summary, diversifying your dividend portfolio is an important strategy for reducing risk and maximizing returns. By investing in a variety of sectors and industries, balancing high-yield and growth dividends, and diversifying within individual sectors and industries, investors can build a diverse and well-rounded portfolio that is more resilient to market fluctuations. By regularly reviewing and rebalancing your portfolio, you can ensure that it remains diversified and well-positioned for long-term success.

Reinvesting Dividends for Maximum Growth

Reinvesting dividends is a strategy that involves using the dividends that a company pays to its shareholders to purchase additional shares of the company's stock. This can be a powerful way to compound returns and maximize growth over the long-term, as the additional shares can generate their own dividends, which can be reinvested in turn.

One of the main benefits of reinvesting dividends is the potential for compound returns. When dividends are reinvested, they can generate additional dividends, which can be reinvested in turn, leading to a cycle of growth. This can be particularly powerful over the long-term, as compound returns can significantly increase the value of an investment.

For example, let's say that you invest $10,000 in a dividend-paying stock that has a dividend yield of 3% and that you reinvest the dividends. Assuming that the stock's price remains constant, after one year, you would have earned $300 in dividends, which you could reinvest to purchase additional shares. After two years, you would have earned $600 in dividends, which you could reinvest to purchase even more shares. This cycle of reinvesting dividends would continue, leading to compound returns that could significantly increase the value of your investment over time.

There are several ways that investors can reinvest dividends. One option is to enroll in a dividend reinvestment plan (DRP) or dividend reinvestment and stock purchase plan (DRSP). These plans allow investors to automatically reinvest their dividends in additional shares of the company's stock, rather than receiving the dividends in cash.

Many companies offer DRPs or DRSPs to their shareholders, and they can be a convenient and cost-effective way to reinvest dividends.

Another option is to reinvest dividends manually, by using the dividends to purchase additional shares of the company's stock on the open market. Manually reinvesting dividends can give investors more control over the process, as they can decide when and how to make their purchases. However, it is important for investors to be aware of any fees or commissions associated with manually reinvesting dividends, as these can eat into returns.

It is also important for investors to consider their overall investment strategy when reinvesting dividends. While reinvesting dividends can be a powerful way to compound returns and maximize growth, it may not always be the best option. For example, investors who are in a high tax bracket or who have immediate cash needs may prefer to receive their dividends in cash, rather than reinvesting them. In these cases, it may be more beneficial for investors to use their dividends to meet their current financial needs and save or invest the cash in other ways.

Reinvesting dividends can be a powerful tool for maximizing growth and compounding returns over the long-term. By understanding the benefits and risks of this strategy, and by considering their overall investment goals and needs, investors can make informed decisions and determine whether reinvesting dividends is the right choice for them.

Tax considerations for dividend investors

As a dividend investor, it's important to understand the tax implications of your investment strategy. Dividends are typically taxable as ordinary income, which means they are subject to the same tax rates as your salary or other earned income. However, there are a few key things you should be aware of when it comes to taxes and dividends.

First, it's important to know that not all dividends are taxed at the same rate. Qualified dividends, which are dividends paid by domestic or qualifying foreign corporations, are taxed at a lower rate than ordinary dividends. To qualify as a qualified dividend, the stock must be held for a certain period of time, typically more than 60 days during the 121-day period that begins 60 days before the ex-dividend date.

If you receive non-qualified dividends, such as dividends from real estate investment trusts (REITs) or master limited partnerships (MLPs), they are taxed as ordinary income at your marginal tax rate.

Another important tax consideration for dividend investors is the impact of dividend income on your overall tax bracket. Depending on your income level, dividend income can push you into a higher tax bracket, which could result in a higher overall tax liability. This is something to keep in mind if you have a significant amount of dividend income, as it could impact your tax planning.

There are a few strategies that you can use to minimize your tax liability as a dividend investor. One strategy is to invest in tax-efficient funds, such as index funds or ETFs (as suggested earlier), which tend to generate fewer taxable capital gains and dividends than actively-managed funds. Another strategy is to hold your dividend-paying stocks in a tax-advantaged account, such as a 401(k) or IRA, which can help to defer or eliminate taxes on your dividend income.

You can also consider investing in stocks that pay dividends that are taxed at the lower qualified dividends rate. As mentioned earlier, qualified dividends are taxed at a lower rate than ordinary dividends, so investing in stocks that pay qualified dividends can help to lower your overall tax liability.

It's also a good idea to review your portfolio on a regular basis and consider selling stocks that have appreciated in value and generating a capital gain. By realizing capital gains in a year when you have lower income, you may be able to take advantage of lower tax rates.

Finally, it's important to keep good records of your dividend income and any tax-related documents. This can help you accurately report your dividend income on your tax return and ensure that you are paying the correct amount of taxes.

Managing risk in a dividend portfolio

it's important to manage risk in your portfolio to help ensure the long-term success of your investment strategy. There are several strategies that you can use to minimize risk and protect your portfolio from volatility and market downturns.

One of the most effective strategies for managing risk in a dividend portfolio is diversification. By investing in a diverse range of dividend-paying stocks, you can spread your risk across different sectors and industries, which can help to reduce volatility and mitigate the impact of any individual stock's performance. Diversification can be achieved through investing in a variety of dividend-paying stocks directly, or through investing in dividend-focused mutual funds or ETFs, which offer the benefits of professional management and diversification.

Another strategy for managing risk in a dividend portfolio is to avoid over-concentration in any one stock or industry. This means not putting too much of your portfolio into any one stock or sector, as this can increase your risk of losing money if that stock or sector performs poorly. Instead, aim to build a well-balanced portfolio that includes a mix of stocks and sectors, and regularly review your portfolio to ensure that it remains diversified.

It's also important to maintain a long-term perspective when it comes to dividend investing. While it's natural to be concerned about short-term market fluctuations, it's important to remember that dividends are a long-term investment. By holding onto your dividend-paying stocks for an extended period of time, you can potentially benefit from compound returns and the potential for capital appreciation.

In addition to these core strategies, there are also a few other tactics that you can use to help manage risk in a dividend portfolio.

One tactic is to use stop-loss orders, which are orders to sell a stock if it falls below a certain price. This can help to protect your portfolio from steep declines in the value of individual stocks. Another tactic is to use options or other derivatives to hedge against risk or enhance returns, although these strategies can be complex and carry their own risks.

PART THREE

Advanced Strategies for Experienced Investors

As an experienced investor, you may be interested in exploring more advanced strategies for maximizing the potential returns and minimizing the risk of your dividend investments. One such strategy is the use of options, which are financial derivatives that give you the right, but not the obligation, to buy or sell an underlying security at a specific price (the strike price) on or before a certain date (the expiration date).

There are two main types of options: call options and put options. Call options give you the right to buy the underlying security, while put options give you the right to sell the underlying security. Options can be used for a variety of purposes, such as to generate income, hedge against risk, or speculate on the direction of a security's price.

1. One way that experienced investors can use options in a dividend-focused portfolio is to sell call options against their dividend-paying stocks. This strategy, known as a covered call, involves selling call options on stocks that you own, while retaining the underlying shares. By selling call options, you are effectively collecting a premium from the buyer of the option in exchange for agreeing to sell your stock at a predetermined price (the strike price) if the option is exercised.

The covered call strategy can be a useful way to generate additional income from your dividend-paying stocks, as the premium you collect from selling the call option can provide an additional source of income. This strategy can also help to hedge against the risk of a decline in the stock's price, as you retain the underlying shares and any dividends they may pay.

2. Another advanced strategy for experienced investors is the use of dividend collar options. A dividend collar involves selling call options and using the proceeds to purchase put options on the same underlying stock. By selling calls and buying puts, you are effectively "collaring" the stock, limiting your potential upside while also protecting against a decline in the stock's price.

This strategy can be a useful way to generate income from your dividend-paying stocks while also hedging against downside risk. It's important to note, however, that using options involves additional risks, such as the risk of loss on the option's premium if the option expires worthless.

In addition to options, there are several other derivatives that experienced investors may consider using in a dividend-focused portfolio. These include futures, swaps, and forwards, which can be used to speculate on the direction of a security's price or to hedge against risk.

It's important to note that using derivatives carries additional risks and may not be suitable for all investors. Derivatives can be complex financial instruments, and it's important to have a thorough understanding of how they work before incorporating them into your investment strategy. It may also be helpful to consult with a financial professional or seek the advice of a financial advisor before using derivatives.

3. Another advanced strategy that experienced investors may consider is the use of dividend capture strategies. Dividend capture strategies involve buying and selling stocks around the ex-dividend date (the date on which a stock's dividend is no longer "owned" by the holder of the stock) in order to capture the dividend without holding the stock for the required holding period.

There are a few different ways to implement a dividend capture strategy, such as buying the stock just before the ex-dividend date and selling it shortly after, or selling short the stock just before the ex-dividend date and buying it back after the dividend has been paid.

While dividend capture strategies can provide the opportunity to generate quick profits, they also carry additional risks, such as the risk of missing the dividend if the trade doesn't execute as planned, or the risk of a decline in the stock's price if the trade goes against you. It's important to carefully consider the risks and potential rewards of any dividend capture strategy before implementing it in your portfolio.

4. Another advanced strategy that experienced investors may consider is the use of dividend arbitrage. Dividend arbitrage involves buying a stock before the ex-dividend date and selling a related derivative, such as a call option or a futures contract, to capture the dividend. This strategy can be used to generate additional income from the dividend, but it also carries the risk of loss if the trade does not execute as planned.

Case studies and real-world examples

It can be helpful to learn from the experiences and strategies of other successful dividend investors. By studying real-world examples and case studies, you can gain valuable insights and ideas for your own dividend investing approach.

1. One example of a successful dividend investor is Warren Buffett, the legendary investor and CEO of Berkshire Hathaway. Buffett is known for his long-term, value-oriented approach to investing, and he has made a fortune by investing in high-quality, dividend-paying stocks. Some of the dividend-paying stocks in Berkshire

Hathaway's portfolio include IBM, Coca-Cola, and Johnson & Johnson.

2. Another successful dividend investor is John Bogle, the founder of Vanguard and a pioneer of index fund investing. Bogle is a strong believer in the power of dividends as a source of long-term return, and he has advocated for the importance of building a diversified portfolio of dividend-paying stocks.

One specific case study of a successful dividend investment is Procter & Gamble (P&G), a consumer goods company that has a long history of paying dividends. P&G has consistently increased its dividends for over 60 years, and it has a track record of generating strong returns for shareholders.

One strategy that P&G has used to increase its dividends is through share buybacks. By reducing the number of outstanding shares, P&G has been able to increase the amount of its profits that are available to be paid out as dividends. This has helped to drive dividend growth and increase returns for shareholders.

3. Another example of a successful dividend investment is McDonald's, a fast food company that has a long history of paying dividends. McDonald's has consistently increased its dividends for over 40 years, and it has a track record of generating strong returns for shareholders.

One strategy that McDonald's has used to increase its dividends is through strong financial performance. The company has consistently reported strong profits, which has enabled it to increase its dividends and return value to shareholders.

4. Another successful dividend investment is Johnson & Johnson, a healthcare company that has a long history of paying dividends. Johnson & Johnson has consistently increased its dividends for over 60 years, and it has a track record of generating strong returns for shareholders.

One strategy that Johnson & Johnson has used to increase its dividends is through strong financial performance. The company has consistently reported strong profits, which has enabled it to increase its dividends and return value to shareholders.

In addition to its financial performance, Johnson & Johnson has also benefited from a diverse product portfolio and a strong brand reputation. The company operates in a variety of healthcare sectors, including pharmaceuticals, medical devices, and consumer products, which has helped to diversify its revenue streams and mitigate risk.

5. Another successful dividend investor is Peter Lynch, the former manager of the Fidelity Magellan Fund and a well-known author and investor. Lynch is known for his growth-oriented approach to investing, and he has made a fortune by investing in high-quality, growing companies that pay dividends.

One specific case study of a successful dividend investment according to Lynch's approach is PepsiCo, a consumer goods company that has a long history of paying dividends. PepsiCo has consistently increased its dividends for over 40 years, and it has a track record of generating strong returns for shareholders.

One strategy that PepsiCo has used to increase its dividends is through strong financial performance and a focus on shareholder value. The company has consistently reported strong profits, and it has implemented share buyback programs and increased its dividend payout ratio in order to return value to shareholders.

In addition to its financial performance, PepsiCo has also benefited from a diverse product portfolio and a strong brand reputation. The company operates in a variety of consumer goods sectors, including beverages, snacks, and food, which has helped to diversify its revenue streams and mitigate risk.

6. Another successful dividend investor is Philip Fisher, a well-known investor and author who is known for his growth-oriented approach to investing. Fisher believed that it was important to invest in high-quality companies with strong growth prospects, and he often looked for companies that paid dividends as a sign of financial stability and management's confidence in the company's future prospects.

One specific case study of a successful dividend investment according to Fisher's approach is Intel, a technology company that has a long history of paying dividends. Intel has consistently increased its dividends for over 25 years, and it has a track record of generating strong returns for shareholders.

One strategy that Intel has used to increase its dividends is through strong financial performance and a focus on shareholder value. The company has consistently reported strong profits, and it has implemented share buyback programs and increased its dividend payout ratio in order to return value to shareholders.

In addition to its financial performance, Intel has also benefited from a strong market position and a diversified product portfolio. The company is a leader in the semiconductor industry, and it produces a wide range of microprocessors and other technology products for a variety of end markets. This has helped to diversify its revenue streams and mitigate risk.

7. Another successful dividend investor is Bill Nygren, a portfolio manager at Oakmark Funds and a well-known value investor. Nygren is known for his focus on finding undervalued companies with strong growth

prospects, and he often looks for companies that pay dividends as a sign of financial stability and management's confidence in the company's future prospects.

One specific case study of a successful dividend investment according to Nygren's approach is Microsoft, a technology company that has a long history of paying dividends. Microsoft has consistently increased its dividends for over 20 years, and it has a track record of generating strong returns for shareholders.

One strategy that Microsoft has used to increase its dividends is through strong financial performance and a focus on shareholder value. The company has consistently reported strong profits, and it has implemented share buyback programs and increased its dividend payout ratio in order to return value to shareholders.

In addition to its financial performance, Microsoft has also benefited from a strong market position and a diversified product portfolio. The company is a leader in the technology industry, and it produces a wide range of software and hardware products for a variety of end markets. This has helped to diversify its revenue streams and mitigate risk.

8. Another successful dividend investor is Benjamin Graham, the "father of value investing" and a well-known investor and author. Graham believed that it was important to invest in undervalued companies with strong financial fundamentals, and he often looked for companies that paid dividends as a sign of financial stability and management's confidence in the company's future prospects.

One specific case study of a successful dividend investment according to Graham's approach is Pfizer, a healthcare company that has a long history of paying dividends. Pfizer has consistently increased its dividends for over 25 years, and it has a track record of generating strong returns for shareholders.

One strategy that Pfizer has used to increase its dividends is through strong financial performance and a focus on shareholder value. The company has consistently reported strong profits, and it has implemented share buyback programs and increased its dividend payout ratio in order to return value to shareholders.

In addition to its financial performance, Pfizer has also benefited from a diverse product portfolio and a strong brand reputation. The company operates in a variety of healthcare sectors, including pharmaceuticals, consumer healthcare, and animal health, which has helped to diversify its revenue streams and mitigate risk.

9. Another successful dividend investor is Howard Marks, the co-founder of Oaktree Capital Management and a well-known value investor. Marks is known for his emphasis on risk management and his focus on finding undervalued companies with strong growth prospects. He often looks for companies that pay dividends as a sign of financial stability and management's confidence in the company's future prospects.

One specific case study of a successful dividend investment according to Marks' approach is Cisco Systems, a technology company that has a long history of paying dividends. Cisco has consistently increased its dividends for over 20 years, and it has a track record of generating strong returns for shareholders.

One strategy that Cisco has used to increase its dividends is through strong financial performance and a focus on shareholder value. The company has consistently reported strong profits, and it has implemented share buyback programs and increased its dividend payout ratio in order to return value to shareholders.

In addition to its financial performance, Cisco has also benefited from a strong market position and a diversified product portfolio. The company is a leader in the networking and communication technology industry, and it produces a wide range of products and services for a variety of end markets. This has helped to diversify its revenue streams and mitigate risk.

Overall, there are numerous examples of successful dividend investors and specific dividend-paying stocks that have generated strong returns for shareholders. By studying these real-world examples and case studies, you can gain valuable insights and ideas for your own dividend investing strategy.

www.ingramcontent.com/pod-product-compliance
Lightning Source LLC
Chambersburg PA
CBHW070310220526
45465CB00004B/1832